C000021366

All Materials in this book © 2019 Jeff Coffin

www.jeffcoffin.com

www.earuprecords.com

Writing & Art by Jeff Coffin, Edited by Charlotte Belyae

Covers by Robert Hakalski, Layout by Morgan Slone

Dedicated to the memory of Kofi Burbridge

One of the greatest musical presences I have ever encountered. You left a deep void when you left us and we will fill it with sound. Thank you for being a part of so many of us...

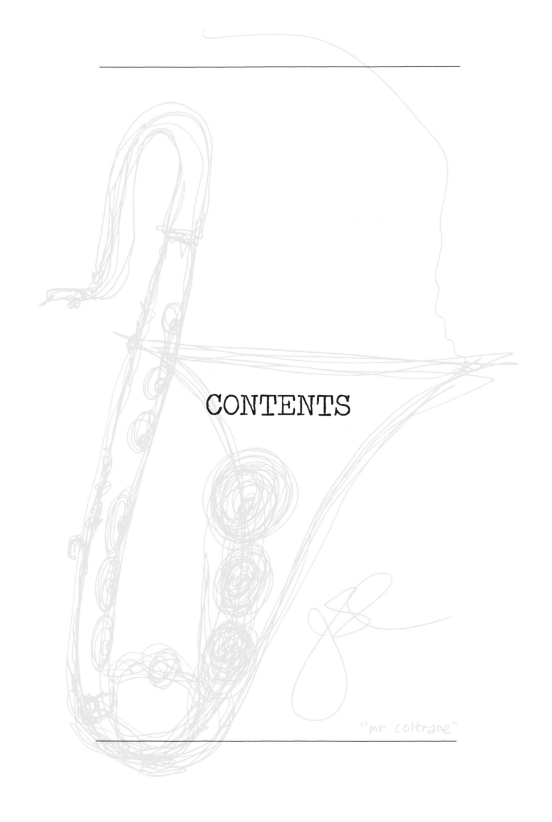

CONTENTS

"mr. coltrane"

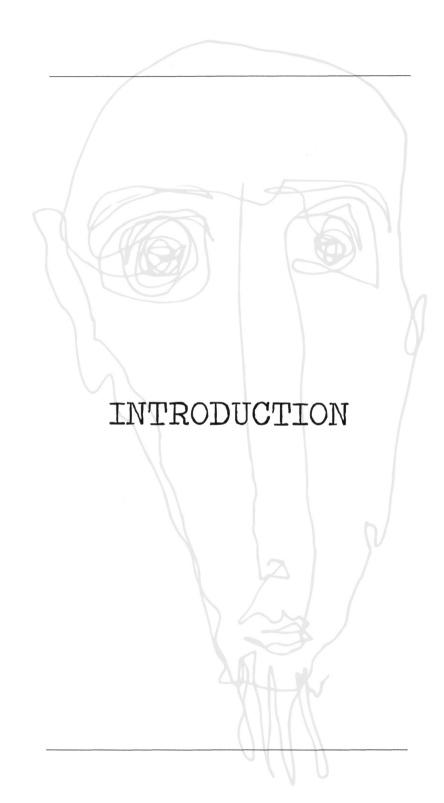

INTRODUCTION

Yes, this is a real book... not a "Real Book." But, yea, it's a real book! I hope the information here will help you further your career in a positive and realistic way. I know it did with mine. Ok, on with the show...

Soooooooo, you want to be a touring musician. You want to get out on the road, make some great music, have some good laughs, eat some great food, and please some people. I get it. That was one of my goals when I was a young musician too! It still is. When I graduated from the University of North Texas I wanted to be out making music, surviving on the road with other musicians, and 'living the dream!!'

You feel you've got the passion, the willingness, the desire, and the drive, and you want to go out and see what life on the road is really like. Right on! I've been fortunate to have a career full of great music, musicians, and memories. I've learned a lot along the way and I'd like to share some of my knowledge and experience with you. And, of course, I wish you all the success you can possibly imagine!

But wait, you might ask, isn't there more to being a successful musician than just having the passion, willingness, desire, and drive? Great question! For sure there is. You have to be organized, articulate, easy to work with, have self-evaluation skills, and a lot more. The road isn't an easy place to thrive and survive, and there are many things to think about before (and after) you leave the driveway with your band. The purpose of this book is to address 'before' parts. The road presents many fluid situations on a daily basis and it will take your best self to deal with them. It's a lot like improvising, where the surprise and unexpected await you at every turn. If you can't already, you'll have to learn to go with the flow. For some, it can be a steep learning curve but you'll figure it out soon enough. Hopefully, this tiny, little book will help you with that.

When I first started out, I had a lot of questions... What's the road like? How do I get on it? Who do I take with me? How do I get where I'm going? How do I get back? What are some steps to booking my own gigs? What are some creative ways of being creative on the road? How do I make financial ends meet and come back with money in my pocket? How do I decide how many players to take, or how much I can pay them? Who will be in my band? What's a rider? How do I deal with merchandise? Do I need a road manager? What do I need for merchandise, how do I get it, and much does it cost? How do I deal with press and promo? How do I figure out a budget before I leave? What about contracts? What about the van rental? What do I include in an itinerary?

HELP MEEEEEEEEEEEEEEEEEEEEEEEEEEEEEEEE...

These are just some of the questions, with real-life suggestions, that I will be covering here. What you're holding in your artistic hand is **The Road Book: A Musician's Guide: How To Navigate The Road (Before You Even Leave The Driveway!).** This book includes lots of things to think about along your way, as well as a few of my professional and personal suggestions (like make a budget before leaving, and don't eat lots of fast food on the road!)

Some topics I cover will be common sense, and maybe trivial-sounding, but they are important to think about. Other topics are more conceptual and esoteric and will require you to figure out your own answers and your own way through.

I won't lie — sometimes, it's tough. These are all things I have had to deal with, professionally and personally over the years in many different ways, with many different people, and in many different configurations and situations. I hope this book helps you find success in your road experience and career.

Let's start at the beginning...

This is when you find yourself sitting at the kitchen table staring blankly out the window, daydreaming about how great it's gonna be to finally get on the road! Or, you may find yourself thinking about all the things you have to do to get ready for the tour. Or you may just be thinking about lunch. That was me. Ok, I was actually all of the above. Here are some of the things I suggest you think about and deal with before you leave your driveway on tour...

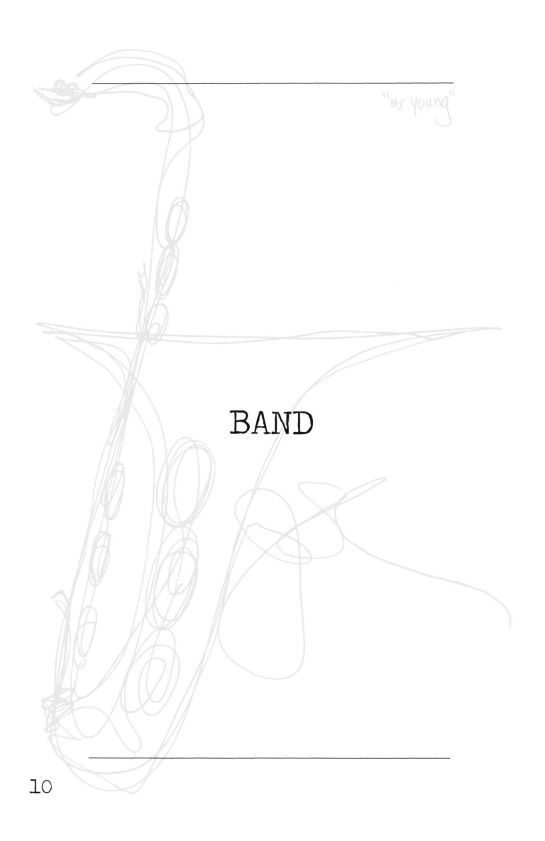

"mr. young"

BAND

01 Do you have a band?

Silly question? Nope. It may sound like a no-brainer but it may just be the most important question in the book.

Are you a solo act or do you have band members? What expectations do you have of your bandmates? Are they even willing to go on the road? Are there any existing personal or professional issues within the group? Being on the road can magnify a small and seemingly insignificant issue tenfold. No one is perfect so you can't expect that, but you should be able to expect professionalism, kindness, and an even-keeled personality.

Communicate kindly, openly, and honestly with your band, in a non- confrontational way, about your expectations and the job description. Have a conversation. Or ten. Remember, it's ALL about relationships. Develop strong bonds with people and those relationships will last a lifetime.

02 Who do you hire?

This seems simple, and it might be, but here are some things to consider. Are the players you are working with easy to be around? Are there any bad feelings or attitudes or even addiction issues that might get in the way of doing what you are trying to do? Can you deal with being in a van with these people for hours, days, and even weeks or months at a time? Providing both can play the music, is it better to hire the best player or the best person?

Consider that gigs will likely be 2 to 3 hours a night. That makes it 21 to 22 hours every day you have to be around these other people. Is hanging out with them fun? Are they considerate of other peoples' space and needs? Consider their disposition and attitude before you hire them.

03 What kind of music do you want to play?

What kind of music moves you? What are you and your band passionate about playing? Don't make it only about getting a paycheck because, at first, those might be hard to come by. Play the music you love and have a passion for. Money is important though because you have to eat, buy gas, get to the next gig, and pay the musicians!

Try to find a healthy balance between playing the music you love and getting paid. A good friend once said there is a big difference between free and fair. Musicians deserve to get paid while they are on the road working hard. Figure out how that can happen for you.

Do you want to be in small clubs playing intimate improvisational music or do you want to be in large theaters playing in a slightly less intimate setting? Give some thought to how your music translates to different audiences and venues. There is nothing wrong with thinking big and there is nothing wrong with keeping it small. It's your career and you get to make the decisions.

04 Do you have music to play?

Who is writing the music you'll be playing? Is your band a 'cover' band? Is it all original music? What about charts... who writes them? If you're paying someone to put your music into a music notation program to print, that's a significant cost to consider.

Who will make folders for the band? Don't forget to include the cost of printing, and however you will store the music, in your budget. It's all part of the cost of doing business. Will you ask your band to memorize all the music? I recommend that for sure but it's not always feasible. If you're printing music, I suggest putting it into plastic sheet protectors and 3-ring binders to protect it and keep it in one place.

Do you have your publishing taken care of? If not, you should have an affiliation with BMI or ASCAP so you can earn money on original music you play live. Look them up online, connect, and ask questions. Make sure you have clarity before signing anything.

05 Who is your audience?

I have found that, almost without exception, everyone loves music! Find out who your audience is. Is it young people? Old people? All ages of people? What's the demographic of your audience? Find places and venues where you can reach people who will like your music. For example, playing jazz in a small country music club in rural Montana might not be the best place for you. You should search out appropriate venues for your music.

Music can cross all boundaries and all age groups and you should try to reach as many people as you can through the music you play and write. After all, it's about emotionally connecting with the people who support you. You have to give them a reason to come and then to come back again. Bottom line... play great music and people will appreciate it and come to hear you. Don't be discouraged if it takes a while to get people to your shows. It's all a process with lots of highs and lows.

06 What if some of your players are suddenly unavailable to tour?

Ok, a week before the tour, your drummer cancels. Obviously, You can't cancel the gig or tour. What do you do? Can you find a sub to fill in? If so, how do you go about finding their replacement? What is the time frame you need to feel comfortable getting them to learn the music? Do you have sheet music? Do you have audio tracks? What type of rehearsing will you have to do? Can they read music? Do they need to be able to read music? What will it cost to bring them out? You might have to pay a little more to bring someone out who can really play the gig right, especially if you're in a bind.

Being the bandleader by yourself is a challenging job and you will have to make some difficult and challenging decisions. Just think about what's best overall for everyone involved and you'll be ok.

07 How do you know when you need a manager?

This is kind of a tough one to answer. It's hard to know exactly when you might need a manager. Ask yourself, what do you need one for? My assistant basically helps me co-manage everything. I bounce a lot of ideas off him and he is my go-between with my booking agent, gig offers, and clinics. He also contracts all my clinics, and represents me to other people. Be sure you have someone you trust who has great people skills, who looks out for your best interests, and who pushes back professionally and politely when necessary. Everyone who's ever dealt with my assistant Brian has only had great things to say about him.

I have other part-time assistants now who help coordinate my schedule, book my hotels and airline flights, help with my website, interviews, get promo out, social media, etc. I don't think I could do this by myself anymore (as I used to) — there are far too many things to get done and I could not do them in a way that I would be satisfied with or find effective. I need the extra help.

Everything takes time, coordination, and effort and it'll always take more time than you expect or want it to. Back to the original question though. If you feel you need a manager more than an assistant, try one. You can expect to pay a manager 10 to 15% of what you make, maybe more. I pay my assistants hourly or by a percentage of the work they bring in.

GIGS

08 What size & type of venue do you want to play?

Deciding the kind of places you want to play can be tricky. Ideally, we would all love to be playing nice venues with great money — but that's not the reality for the most part, especially when you first go on the road. What types of clubs cater to your type of music? Look for touring groups who play a similar style of music as you and approach the clubs they are playing.

Start small and try to get as many people out as possible. A small room that is packed feels much better than a large room with the same crowd. And you can bet clubs prefer a packed room, too! Keep it intimate for a while and move to larger venues as your audience grows.

09 Do you have 'door' gigs or money guarantees?

Obviously, having a guarantee for the gig is much better than depending on the door to make your money. Guarantees help you make a budget and figure out the minimum you'll bring in for the tour. However, it can be hard to get guarantees at first.

Venues are in the business of being in business, and you have to do whatever you can to sell tickets. The main thing clubs want is 'butts in seats.' The venue will do some advertising, but say they have 7 bands a week (or more) — that's over 25 a month and I'm sure you understand how it'd be difficult to make every band a priority in their advertising. It would cost them a fortune and the bottom line is it's not gonna happen. Do what you can to build your audience through social media, interviews with local radio stations and newspapers, press articles, word of mouth, posters, flyers, street teams, etc...

At the end of the night be sure to get the number of people who paid to see you. Higher numbers will give you more leverage to negotiate next time. Ask to have these numbers written down and have a paper trail (email is fine too of course). Do this in a way that benefits you and helps you learn about 'the business of the music business.'

10 Who do you contact at the venues about booking gigs?

A bartender or waitstaff might not be the best person to ask for a gig. Try to find out who the person booking the club is, and be patient. Remember they are trying to run a business and they likely get a lot of inquires daily. No offense, but you are probably just another face to them. Don't take it personally if they are short with you or tell you to call back later.

Be sure to get the correct information to follow up. The follow-up is important! When you do this, be on time, be polite, and be grateful. Be professional and courteous. Have your information together as to when you have availability and are talking money. Regarding money, always ask for more than you hope to make. You can always negotiate down, but you can't ask for more once you've given your price. Just don't be crazy about what you ask for!

11 Do you have signed contracts?

ALWAYS, ALWAYS, ALWAYS have your contracts signed and have a copy with you! Hopefully, this will prevent you from having issues when you're getting paid. If you have no contract and you say you agreed to something and they say something else, you will lose every time. GET IT IN WRITING!

Be sure the information is correct, and 'advance' the gig before you leave or within a few days before the gig. Advancing the gig means to call ahead and talk through any questions you have or any vague details. You will likely have questions about most gigs and getting clarity helps make your experience that much easier. Be sure to talk with the person who signed the contract when possible.

12 Filling out a contract.

Contracts are typically self-explanatory but you should *always* read them thoroughly. If someone wants you to sign something quickly before you can fully read it, or without giving you a copy, you should politely and professionally decline. You are about to be had! Some contracts are more complicated than others and have more restrictions. Starting off, all you really need is a basic contract with information like: payment, gig date, time, set lengths, backline, contact information, hotels, food, parking, etc. Take care of this before you leave. It's super important.

13 Will you be providing your own amps and gear?

This should be assumed but there might be venues where you can use their backline. If you don't know what 'backline' is, it's the gear the venue has that bands can use. The most common is to have a drum set that is the 'house kit.' Maybe a couple of amps too but they are usually pretty lousy. Sometimes the backline is real garbage and sometimes it's ok but rarely is it great. I hope you get lucky and have some good stuff but plan ahead.

Ask for a list of backline equipment to be emailed to you to find out what they have and what might work for you. Sometimes their venue's website will have info too. Ask a lot of questions. I recommend having a checklist of things you need to bring and checking stuff off as you go. Add and subtract gear as you do different tours and find your needs. Using gear that is already at a venue helps with the load in and load out of course, but I recommend using your own stuff because you are familiar with it and you know it actually works.

You should keep a record of all the serial numbers of your gear. Take pictures of it all, too. If anything happens to it, you'll need to be able to identify it.

Look into instrument insurance as well. If you're in the local musicians union they'll be able to provide some information.

14 Making a basic stage plot.

You can use a photograph, an online program, or the like, to put together a basic stage plot to show where everyone will be set up onstage. Be sure to include things like DI (direct input) boxes, microphones, monitor placement, the general set up of the group and where everyone will be. Stage left is to your left if you're onstage looking out toward the audience. Stage right, of course, is the other side. Downstage is behind you if you're looking at the audience. Upstage is in front of you, closest to the crowd.

Include your email and phone number on the plot. Have a pdf so you can send it easily through email and be sure it's not too large of a file. Make it easy and clear to read so the audio person isn't trying to decipher a crazy hieroglyphic-looking sketch. Be clear and concise and it will always help you. It helps the club too.

15 Will you bring someone to run sound?

If you can afford to do this, DO! Sonic consistency (it looks cool to write that) is an important part of the overall sound of a group. It's not always possible to bring someone to run sound, so most times you'll be at the mercy of whoever the club brings in. This may or may not prove to be positive. Sometimes it's great. Other times, maybe most times, not so much.

If you are unable to bring your own sound person, be sure to communicate your needs and wants with the person there. If you feel the room is too loud when you soundcheck, be as professional, polite, and clear as possible. You want them on your side!! They can be your best friend or worst enemy during the show depending on the communication level and relationship you establish early.

Learn their name. Introduce them to the rest of the band. Be patient, kind, and thankful for their help. You are likely just another band to them and they work hard too. Be firm, but polite, if you need some-thing you are not getting. It's important that you're comfortable with the sound even though you can be sure it will never be perfect. Communication is key. Early on in my career I was sometimes harder on some sound people than I should've been. I wasn't the most patient person and hated getting 'spiked' by feedback. Still do. Only now, I can't really hear it anymore! (Just kidding.) Thank them at the end of the night and onstage if you're comfortable doing that. Everyone appreciates a shout out.

16 Will venues provide meals?

This is something you can ask for on your 'rider,' if there is one. A rider is a list of what you'd like to have at the venue. Things like, snacks, drinks, fruit, dinner, etc... Having dinner at the gig saves quite a lot of money during the time you are on the road. FREE FOOD!! You can usually specify what type of food you want.

Sometimes you can request a buy-out, where the venue gives you $15 to $25 each for dinner rather than providing it themselves. Use common sense, don't be greedy with your requests. Don't ask for clean socks or green M&M's. At least not at first. :)

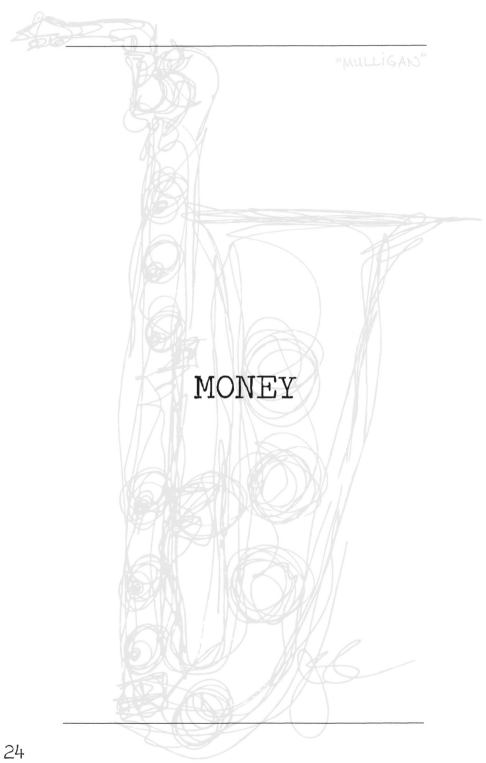

MONEY

17 How much will you pay everyone in the group?

This, of course, depends on your guarantees and your overall budget after expenses such as hotels, gas, manager/assistant fees, booking agent fees, etc. This is one of the most difficult expenses to decide.

Let me give an example: after expenses, you have $4000 left over for a week on the road, and 5 people to pay (including yourself). How much can you afford to pay everyone? If you divide $4000 by 5 people, that's $800 each. Not a terrible week, but certainly not great. It's a little over $100 per day. But what happens if you have any additional expenses along the way? What if you want to take the band out for drinks, or to buy them breakfast one morning? If you paid everyone $700 for the week instead, you'd have $500 'extra' to put toward added expenses. Or you could put it into a band account, so down the road when you DO have extra expenses, you've got it covered. You could consider this an Emergency Fund.

Paying the band will vary, of course. You'll have to figure out what works best for you and the people playing with you. I pay my band as much as possible because they deserve it and I want them to feel good about being on the road. Talk with each person about what you can afford, and give them a guarantee for the trip before you leave. If you can pay more after, that's a bonus! Extra money is always appreciated, and it makes you feel good giving it to the musicians who have just done their best for you. Good luck!

18 Who will settle up after the gig?

...as in, who gets the dough?! RULE #1: BE SURE YOU HAVE A SIGNED CONTRACT! Who will collect the band's money from the club? Find out before the gig who you need to settle the contract with at the end of the show. Have a signed contract when collecting to be sure that everything is correct and you're collecting everything you're entitled to. Know this info in advance! If they say they sent a deposit and you are unaware of that, ask for some type of proof. If cash was promised on the contract, be sure to get what they're obligated to pay. It may sound crazy, but club owners have been known to take advantage of bands and musicians, and you must be your own advocate.

Gently, politely, firmly, and professionally take care of business. Be prepared for some difficulties and be aware you will need to think on your feet sometimes. I have been burned a few times and it will likely happen to you along the way. It sucks, but it'll probably happen no matter how thorough you are. Remember, you have to learn the business of being in the music business. It's a process.

19 Where will you keep the money you collect?

A crumpled wad of cash in your suitcase or bag isn't the best place for your money. I recommend getting some of those money pouches with zippers from an office supply store, like banks use. Some even have a lock and heavy-duty zippers. Designate one responsible person who will hold the money. I think it should always be the leader — that way, if something happens, it's the leader's responsibility. Either way, whoever collects and carries the money is the one accountable for it.

Write down what you collect every night and be sure your counting is correct. Count the money twice when you collect and count it both times in front of who just paid you. If you wait to count it in the van and it's not the right amount, you're out of luck and you just got taken to the cleaners. Welcome to the seedy side of the music business! Don't leave money in the van or sitting out in the hotel room. If you are giving cash advances to the band be sure to write it down when you give the advance. Don't wait, you WILL forget. A small amount of work goes a long way in keeping your finances together and you will be thankful you did the work. It's yet another part of being a band leader.

20 What are your possible miscellaneous expenses?

You will encounter unexpected touring-related expenses and you should try to 'guesstimate' these miscellaneous expenses into your budget. What happens if when you have to get an extra hotel room, gas goes up, you break down, you go North instead of South for an hour or two and have to buy more gas, you spend more money on food than expected, your gear breaks, you need new wiper blades, your brakes start making terrible noises, etc.? Be able to roll with these things and learn to expect the unexpected.

Oh, and don't forget that if you have a booking agent, manager, or assistant, you can expect to pay them between 10% to 15% of your gig and/or clinic money. Do the math and be sure you have it all right. Check it a couple times. Go over it with your bandmates, assistant, manager, or booking agent before your leave your driveway.

21 Paying for expenses on the road...

If possible, I recommend getting a business credit card so all your professional and business expenses go onto it. If you get one that has airline rewards points, you'll be able to save money on flights and maybe even get free ones from time to time. Some have cash back. Do the research and decide which one is right for you. It will help you establish better credit too. If you cannot get a business card, get a regular one you ONLY use for business. Mark it so you remember it's only being used for business.

This is also good at tax time so you know what your individual business expenses were. Using Quicken, Quickbooks, or another expense/tax program can help you keep track of your specific personal and professional expenses.

TRAVEL

22 What roles are people given on the road?

  I suggest you ask your band if they are open to being given responsibilities on the road other than just playing the gig. If you are starting out or road managing yourself this would take a lot of burden off you. You can tell them that by not having to pay an extra person they would actually get paid more. Some will like the idea, others may not. You might offer to pay one person extra to take on an assistant role on the road. If you do this, you're only dealing with one other person rather than the whole group.

  Their duties may be as simple as helping unload the van, counting merchandise in and out, texting rooming lists and van 'call' time (meaning the time you are leaving), helping with routing, pumping gas, etc...

  Having help can take a lot of stress and pressure from your day to day and it allows others to get a little more experience of what it's like to be on the road with responsibilities other than playing the gig. I can say from experience, however, this doesn't always work. You should deal with it on a situation-by-situation basis.

23 How will you be traveling?

  Do you own an old bus, van, camper, RV, etc...? If you own your vehicle, be sure it's reliable. Safety is the #1 most important thing on the road. Everyone is responsible for everyone else. Don't take chances with anyone's life. Get good tires and wiper blades that work; get oil changes regularly and be sure the brakes are solid.

What happens if your vehicle breaks down? Do you have roadside assistance, AAA, or auto insurance? Figure out how these expenses will be covered and be sure everyone is in agreement. Finances about things like this can be complicated and there will usually be more than one discussion about it. A tip on insurance: If you have an LLC (Limited Liability Corporation), you can get a commercial license plate for your touring vehicle and register it as such. The commercial insurance can usually be taken off when you're not on the road, which will save you a bundle of money! Just be sure to reactivate the insurance before you leave again!!

24 How much is a rental van?

If you don't own a van and have to rent one, how much is it? Where will you return it? How much are additional drivers? Do you have to pay insurance? How much is that? Be sure your rental includes un-limited mileage. You'll have to do some homework to find the best deal. Ask around to see if you know someone with a van they aren't using and see if you can rent it. Maybe even mine! (Not really.) Be sure you have insurance and that the insurance company knows what's up.

Keeping the van clean is an essential everyday/everybody chore. Nobody wants to find half of a sandwich a week after the other half was eaten. Get rid of your trash and take care of your personal surroundings. Van smells don't go away by themselves... trust me.

25 How much is your gas expense?

This is essential to figure out for your budget. I always figure out approximately how many miles I'll be traveling and how much gas will cost BEFORE I leave the driveway. This can be done by making an itinerary and knowing how far you'll be going. For example, I know my 15-passenger van loaded with gear gets 14 mpg on the highway. Always round UP on your travel estimate. You'll likely get lost a few times — it's not a road trip until the first U-turn!

26 What happens if your vehicle breaks down?

The obvious answer is, you have to get it fixed. If you blow a tire, you have to know how to put on the spare and find a place that can get you a new tire — or a good used one. If you need repair work done to your vehicle, ask around at the gig to see if someone can recommend a local mechanic. The cheaper you can get it done, the better for your budget. I also highly recommend having some type of roadside assistance. AAA is the standard. I'd suggest the 2nd level, which offers better and further towing options should you ever need it. I hope you don't!

27 How far are you willing to travel per day?

This varies for everyone but I have found 6 hours is about my limit for driving in one day before a gig. Any more than that and the exhaustion of driving and being in a van all day can get a bit much to deal with over time. And usually all the snacks will be gone too. Not cool!

There have been exceptions, on certain days off, that we have driven 15+ hours to get to where we want to be rather than splitting it between a day off and a gig day. We like to stop to enjoy the local scenery as well so we roll that into our travel time. Always be sure to have someone stay awake with whoever is driving. If you're tired, STOP DRIVING! It's not a risk you should take.

28 Will you travel overnight? (NOT recommended!)

I decided a few years ago never to drive overnight again unless we're in a tour bus with a professional driver. There are too many things that can go wrong and it's very, very easy to get tired and fall asleep driving. That would lead to disastrous, and possibly fatal, consequences.

If you're tired and it's late, rest up and drive the next day. It's never worth risking anyone's life for a few more hours of drive time. We sometimes drive an hour or two to the hotel along the route after the gig, but never overnight and never more than 2 hours after the gig. Drive smart and you'll arrive safe. It's also a good idea to gas up your vehicle the night before when possible. Save time when you can.

29 Where will you stay?

Home stays or hotels? Airbnb? Are you comfortable staying on a friend's floor? Do you need individual rooms? Will you camp out? How cheap a hotel can you endure? Lodging is always the largest expense I have on the road. You will have to be smart with your sleeping decisions and chances are pretty good you'll have to double up in rooms at the beginning. Be sure you're clear about this when you talk with your musicians about the gig.

Plan ahead on making reservations and don't wait until right before or even after (!) the gig to figure out where you will be staying. Find an internet site that caters to cheap hotel rooms or call ahead to friends you might be able to stay with. PLAN AHEAD or you'll wish you had. There is nothing worse than not knowing where you are staying and at the end of a long day of driving and playing. The last thing your band wants to hear is "We don't have rooms."

30 What are your lodging expenses?

A clean place to stay is a very important part of the evening and overall morale of the band, but don't stay above what you can afford. How much could you spend on hotel rooms, if you actually get hotel rooms? As I mentioned, doubling up in a room will help keep expenses much lower when you're first starting out. It's not necessarily the best situation, but it will help if you're trying to make ends meet.

You should get into a hotel rewards program and try to find the same hotel chain nightly. At a certain point you will start to get free nights. Choose wisely. Do your research and look at the ratings online.

Call ahead if you'll be checking in late so they don't let your room go. Call ahead to ask for early check-in if you'll be arriving early. Ask the night before, or as early as possible, for a late check-out if you're leaving later than the normal check out time. Most hotels will accommodate when possible. Getting more sleep always helps everyone and the music.

31 Itineraries

This is a very important part of your touring! You need to have itineraries. People have to know things like: specific tour dates, where to go, when to be there, what time to be at soundcheck, where the gig is, what time the gig starts, whether or not dinner is provided, what's in the backline, the venue phone number, the name of the venue's contact person, how to reach that contact by email, the van call time for the next day, how many miles to the next gig, the amount of drive time, the hotel location and phone number, confirmation numbers, flight info, pick up/drop off times, clinic times, transportation arrangements, etc.

Be as specific as possible and it'll help your tour immensely. Don't leave much to chance. Oh, but... realize the band might hardly look at the itinerary and will likely ask you for the information instead! (Hahahaha!) Encourage them to check the itinerary but it's not a bad idea to go over the day's events on the night before. I also encourage group texting with the next day's information for clarity. It may seem redundant, but it'll serve you in the long run and everyone will have the same info. It's kind of like reading the same chart, only without musical notes.

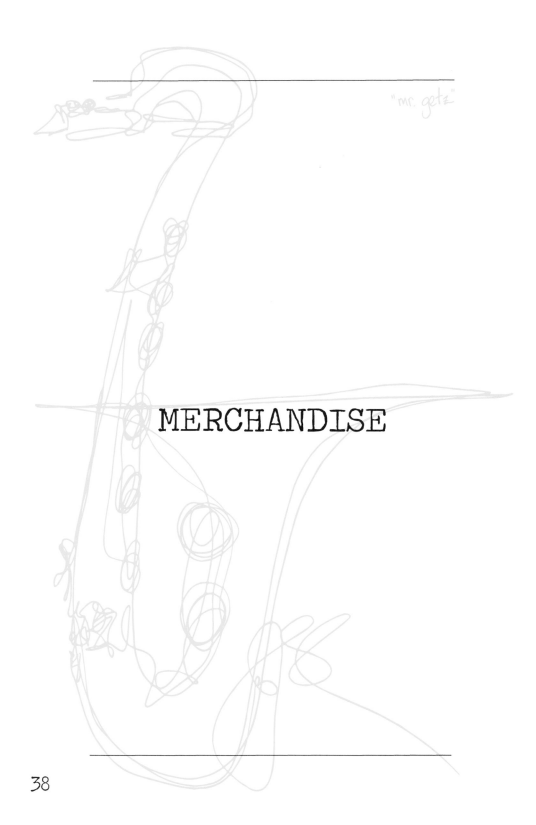

"mr. getz"

MERCHANDISE

32 Do you have merchandise?

Merchandise is an essential revenue stream and a good way to get the word out about your group. Costs are usually low for getting the merchandise and you can set your own selling price once you've got it. What I mean by the cost being low is you can get shirts made up for about $6 to $7 each. You can get hats for about the same (both prices are based on how many you buy).

As far as pricing your merchandise, make a good profit but don't be greedy. When I carry CDs, I usually sell single CDs for $10 to $15 at the gigs and our 2 CD set for $20. If you have about 500 to 1000 made up yourself, you can usually get them for $1 to $2 each. You can get smaller runs too, of course, but the price will go up for smaller runs. If you're making $6 to $8 per CD sale after your initial expense, and you sell 10 to 20 CDs per night, that's pretty good extra money. Every little bit helps!

Bring t-shirts, stickers, hats... etc. Vinyl album costs are different. They're heavier and they take up more space, but many people enjoy them more because they sound better than CDs. Obviously, there are many options.

Don't overload yourself or your merch person, and be thoughtful about what you carry on the road. Having some organization is key to successful merch and there are many ways to do it. Spreadsheets are good. Something like Google Drive is also a good place to store info that is easily accessible.

33 Who pays for merchandise up front?

Is someone willing to put up the money or will it be something that everyone chips into and splits the profits? The business of this can be tricky so be sure you are all very clear on what the agreement is. Writing it out and everyone signing a copy is not a bad thing to have as a record of your agreement. Talk about it and decide what you want to do. If you are a solo artist and have a backup band, that is a different situation and, most likely, you'll be the one dealing with the merchandise and the money from it. If you put money up, you have to get paid back.

You can get a % of merch sales until you recoup your money, or you can get everything until it's all paid for and then the band can split it. Or maybe it's all yours. Again, agree to something and be clear about it with your group. Money can be divisive, and divisiveness isn't good on the road or in friendships.

34 Who will sell your merchandise?

Merchandise has a large profit margin and is one of the best things you can do to help make your tour financially successful. Ask if the venue will provide someone to sell your CDs, shirts, posters, stickers, etc., or, if not, you will have to find a person to sell your merchandise. If you have friends in different cities you might be able to trade tickets to sell merch when you play there. If you don't know anyone you can ask the club if they have anyone they've used before. You might also use social media to find a person. Check with a local college music department — everyone needs a little extra money.

That statement brings up this one: what type of compensation will you give someone who sells for you? Be sure to give them something, even if they say they don't need or want anything. $25 or a piece or two of merchandise is a nice thing to offer. Don't offer too much because you have to stay within a budget but a small token of your gratitude goes a long way. Kindness begets kindness. And, if they did a good job, keep their name for the next time.

Also, and this is important for your success with your merch, have a form you use to keep track of what you have and what you sell. Ideally, you should count in and count out your merch each night. Your numbers should reconcile. Keep a record of what you give away and what you sell. Make your system super easy to use so you're not taking a lot of time every day explaining it to someone. Pretend they know nothing about your inventory system because they actually know nothing about your inventory system. You can put the numbers somewhere like Google Drive or a similar place. These numbers help you know what is and isn't selling. If brown hats are selling twice as much as your black hats, you'll know to buy more brown hats when you reorder. Order small amounts at first. You don't want to spend a ton of money in the beginning but it's important to have stuff to sell. Make that money!!!

35 What's your profit margin on music & merch?

First, you have to figure out what your total music production costs are. This can include: recording, mixing, mastering, artwork, manufacturing vinyl or CDs, shipping, barcodes, ISRC codes, song releases, etc... anything associated with the overall cost of the recording. You can do this type of cost projection with shirts and other merchandise. This may not be completely necessary, but if you're trying to know what you're making as profit, this is part of it.

36 Who makes the posters?

I think this is pretty self-explanatory but, if you have a friend or family member who is a graphic artist, you might ask them to help out. Having their art seen is important and they might be willing to do some gratis (aka free) work at first in hopes that later on you can actually pay them. If you have any money to work with early on, pay them! Anything is better than nothing and I know it's appreciated when someone offers to pay for your creative services.

If you have some graphic design skills, make your own posters. Make a list of all the information that needs to go on them. Look at posters at venues and get some ideas from them. Something cool might help bring people to your show. Try to make something that represents the band. Don't forget to put the date, time, and location of the gig!! (Been there, done that... not good.)

37 How will you get posters to and from the venues?

Do you have a record deal? If so, will they pay for your publicity? If not, it falls on you. If you've hired a publicity person, which is unlikely because they're expensive, they might take care of this. Either way, you should have different poster sizes and designs on your website or social media that the clubs can download and share. I recommend this even if you have someone doing publicity. Have some publicity shots of the group available for download, too, for newpapers and press. If you want color posters, you will probably have to make those up yourself. Clubs likely won't cover the expense of color copies. Black and white posters can be very effective. Make them simple and to the point! Clutter sucks.

Try to gather a 'street team' in different cities that can put posters up. You can put out feelers on social media and find if there are any people interested in coming to the show in exchange for doing some leg work to help promote the gig. Obviously, the more people who know about the gig, the better. There are many ways to get the word out. Use whatever means necessary to let people know about your gig.

Ask your street team to put posters in places that are frequented by people in your demographic. Ask them to hit up social media for you. Be creative with your approach. People appreciate that and it reflects on the whole experience. People love being involved in something cool and fun.

"ERIC DOLPHY"

MARKETING

38 Do you have an online presence?

You'd better! Make sure it's updated, interesting, and easy to navigate. Keep your tour dates and info updated. You might even want to hire someone to help you with this. I did and still do. It has saved me countless hours and is very helpful. Finding someone isn't difficult and it's highly effective for staying on top of things. A simple web page is also easy to put together and you can likely do it yourself to start with. Keep your costs low whenever possible.

39 Use social media to let people know where you are playing.

Social media changes all the time so try to stay on top of what is working and what is not. Obviously, social media is a great way to communicate with a lot of people with very little effort and cost. Ask the venues to post about your gigs and send them info they can post and share. Don't expect them to put a lot of time into thinking about your gig because they won't. It's up to you to do the work. If someone in the band is willing to be in charge and they do it well, let them take it over.

One major thing to be sure you have is a mailing list. People should be able to sign up online or at your gigs (once you have some!). Send out newsletters and get people excited about what's coming up. Content is key but make sure it's good solid content. Have the band collectively, or individually, make a short video inviting people out or maybe video part of a rehearsal to get people excited and interested about the shows. Send links, do some live-streaming, etc...

Don't wait until the last minute and expect people to flock to your gig. Build your brand and sound over time, and be consistent. Give people a reason to come to your shows. Be creative in your approach to reaching people.

40 How do you get in touch with local media?

Get to know some of the local music/arts writers who write for a city's weekly arts guide and local newspapers. Take them out for coffee or invite them to a show. Give them your new CD (don't ask them to pay for it!), or send them digital files or a link to stream. Ask if they would be able to get it to some-one for a review. Maybe they are willing to write an article about the release. If there's a human interest story behind it, let them know. The same goes for radio. They likely have connections outside of the local area just as most musicians do. The circle is small once you're in it.

If you have an assistant or manager, you might have them follow up after you make first contact. You *personally* making first contact is important when possible. It shows initiative and a willingness to reach out to develop a relationship. The value of developing and fostering relationships cannot be overstated in any part of being a musician (or a human being). Your career will likely depend on how well you foster the relationships you make. Don't forget this!

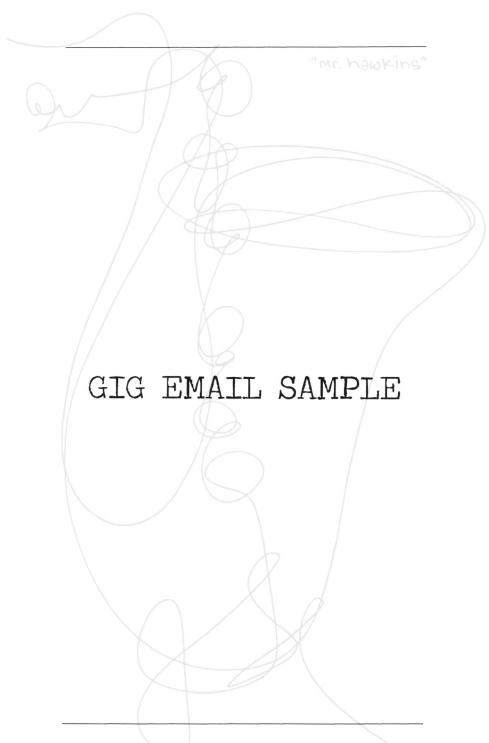

"mr. hawkins"

GIG EMAIL SAMPLE

Just so you know that I put this stuff in this book into practice, here is an e-mail I sent out in January 2019. You'll have to forgive the lack of punctuation and capital letters, this is just how I wrote it. Don't judge me.

This e-mail was for a short 2 day tour. Gig 1 was at Rudy's Jazz Room in Nashville, TN and gig 2 was at the Indianapolis Jazz Kitchen in Indianapolis, IN. You can imagine the complexity and details associated with a longer run. Both gigs included me on saxes, Keith Carlock on drums, Nir Felder on guitar, and Viktor Krauss on acoustic bass. And, this email was one of many that I sent regarding the gigs...

From: Jeff Coffin

hey guys, here is some important info....

please be sure to hit up ur social media with these tix links.
Rudy's - https://bit.ly/2EEflxs
Jazz Kitchen Early Show - https://ticketf.ly/2UVjMhL
Jazz Kitchen Late Show - https://ticketf.ly/2LpYhBw

all the music should be in dropbox now. if there is anything to add please do so ASAP. I just put a new tune in called ABUNDANCE that i'd like to try. there is a loose demo there too. NIR - if u have Bb parts for me on anything i have NOT played before that would be great. everything of mine is on sibelius and should be correct. if anyone needs anything changed or octaves moved, let me know and i'll get it done and repost. my asst julia can also do sibelius charts for anyone. she charges $15 an hour and she's pretty speedy. i am cc'ing her here if interested.

I'm taking alex to indy with us to help with driving the van and whatever other logistics (incl merch sales) we need. he's done tour managing for me and assistant work in the past and he's great! he's a drummer keith, so he can also help with ur gear if u want. i will be paying him $200 and he and i will share a room in indy to keep expenses as low as possible. I am also trying to arrange to have to have someone at rudy's to sell merch. I will slide them a little $$ for doing that. i'm budgeting $30. the total guarantee for each of us on this trip is $XXXX. here is the breakdown of the budget.

RUDY'S JAZZ ROOM:
Guarantee: $XXXX (more if we go into points)
Expenses:
merch seller - $30
Facebook ads - $50
Total expenses: $80
Net Profits: $XXXX
Divided by 4 = $XXXX

INDIANAPOLIS JAZZ KITCHEN:
Guarantee: $XXXX plus hotel
Expenses:
BH commission - $XXXX (BH booked the gig and gets 10%)
Alex - $200 (asst)
Gas - $115 (600mi / 13mpg x $2.50/gal) - gas might be a little more than this per gallon...

Tolls - $5
Total expenses: $570
Net profits: $XXXX
Divided by 4 = $XXXX

the tiny bit left over I will budget for anything misc. like inflated gas prices or the like. please let me know if u have any questions or concerns.

from XXX's: there will be a band, Charles & the Sun Kings, before you guys on that Friday from 5:30 - 7:30. So, I'm not sure what we need to do to make arrangements for soundcheck and all. It will likely need to be a quick 20 minute sound check.
is that doable?? If not, I could maybe have Charles end a little earlier than scheduled to buy you guys a little time? Let me know your thoughts... i'm cool with going in and hitting it!

rough overview:

RUDY'S: (ONE comp tix each)
   7:30 arrive (charles is a great old school soul singer
        and worth a listen if u want to arrive early)
   8pm downbeat
   11pm finish
   2 sets - NOT turning the house.

INDY JAZZ KITCHEN: (will find out about comps)
we should plan to leave from my place on saturday january 5th no later than 8:30am. we lose an hour (going to east coast time) and it's a little over 5 hours to get there not including stops. that gets us there a touch before 3pm or right at 3pm.
   3PM EST - Load-In

4PM EST - Soundcheck
5PM EST - Door open
7:30PM EST - Show 1 (75 minutes)
9PM EST - Doors open
9:30PM EST - Show 2 (75 minutes)

Venue will provide dinner (from club menu) and 4 hotel rooms. At end of the night make sure to pick up check (JC)

Hotel Info - 15 minutes from venue (6.4 miles)
XXX Hotel, Indianapolis, IN 46240

JANUARY 6 - we can leave as early as anyone wants /needs to. alex will be driving so we can all sleep more if need be in the van. oh, and we'll be taking my 15 passenger van. i'll remove the back 2 seats for gear and there will be 2 bench seats and a front seat.

is there anything i'm forgetting? questions? concerns? lemme know. thanks cats! hope this covers everything.

peace, love & happy holidays. jc

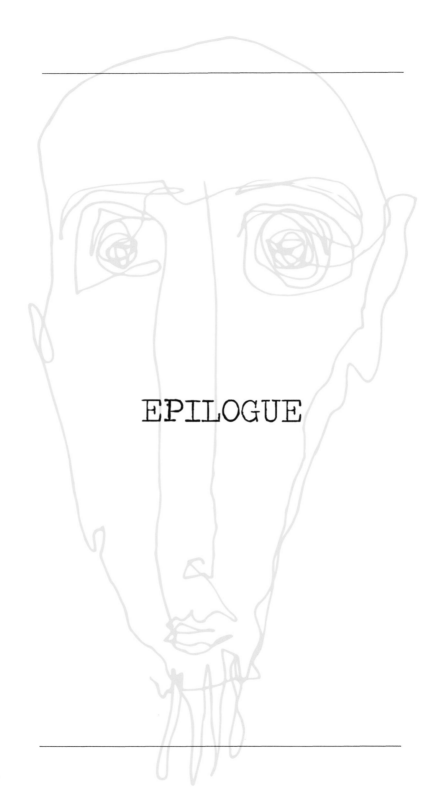

EPILOGUE

So, here we have come to the end of our little discussion about things you should consider before leaving your driveway on tour. Your situation will be a unique situation with its own set of unique issues and unique considerations. There will be unexpected things that come up and you have to be able to think fast and deal with them calmly and professionally in mostly unfamiliar surroundings. And, you will have to lead by example.

As you likely realize, there is a lot more to each of these topics than meets the eye. There is more research you will have to do and you will need to put a lot more hours into touring. It's a hard job but if you really want to do it, I believe these tips will help you along the way. Going into it with your eyes open is important and I hope this information will help you along your journey. I wish you luck and much musical, artistic, financial, and personal success. Safe travels and great gigs!

DEEP THANKS:

Ryoko Suzuki
for her endless love, patience, wisdom, and support

My brothers and sisters on the road
you are truly road warriors

Esmerelda
My van

Charlotte Belyae
for her friendship, editing skills, and extraordinary humor

Brian Horner, Julia Meredith, & Alex Mathews
for their assistance with so many things

Morgan Slone
for her layout skills and being the best niece ever

Yamaha Musical Instruments & D'Addario Woodwinds

All my music educator friends and students

All the other folks who chimed in
with words of wisdom and sagely advice

All the fans
for continuing to support live music and musicians

"CHARLES
LLOYD"

Lightning Source UK Ltd.
Milton Keynes UK
UKHW050627170822
407422UK00003BA/70